The Wisdom of Socrates

Quotes and Insights

Sebastián G.A.

Copyright © Sebastián GA 2024

All rights reserved. No part of this book may be reproduced or transmitted in any form or by any means without written permission from the author.

Under no circumstances will any blame or legal responsibility be held against the publisher or author for any damages, reparation, or monetary loss due to the information contained within this book, either directly or indirectly.

Legal Notice:

This book is copyright-protected. It is only for personal use. You cannot amend, distribute, sell, use, quote, or paraphrase any part or the content within this book without the consent of the author or publisher.

Disclaimer Notice:

Please note the information contained within this document is for educational and entertainment purposes only. All effort has been executed to present accurate, up-to-date, reliable, and complete information. No warranties of any kind are declared or implied. Readers acknowledge that the author is not engaged in the rendering of legal, financial, medical, or professional advice. The content within this book has been derived from various sources. Please consult a licensed professional before attempting any techniques outlined in this book.

By reading this document, the reader agrees that under no circumstances is the author responsible for any losses, direct or indirect, that are incurred as a result of the use of the information contained within this document, including, but not limited to, errors, omissions, or inaccuracies.

Table of Contents

Acknowledgments i

Message from the Author 1

Introduction 2

Chapter 1: On Knowledge and Ignorance 3

Chapter 2: On Life and Self-Improvement 11

Chapter 3: On Ethics and Virtue 25

Chapter 4: On Love and Relationships 38

Chapter 5: On Courage and Strength 45

Chapter 6: On Death and the Immortality of the Soul 53

Chapter 7: On God and the Divine Order 56

Chapter 8: Life and Background 62

    Early Life 62

    Military Service 62

    Philosophical Pursuits 62

    Trial and Death 63

    Legacy 63

    Philosophical Method 63

    Connections With Other Philosophers 64

Conclusion 65

About the Author 66

References 67

Acknowledgments

Thank you, Shake Shake. Without your existence, I wouldn't be the human I am today. This first book is thanks to you. Andele!

Be the kind of person your dog thinks you are.

-J.W. Stephens

Further acknowledgment to B.K. Hanifah for the impeccable book cover design. I truly appreciate your time, talent, and skills. (@bkhgraphic: Instagram)

Message from the Author

Welcome! Thank you for opening this small book filled with quotes by my favorite philosopher. I encourage all who read it to reflect on some of the quotes and use my explanations to get a personal feel for how to apply the quotes. In some cases, I will encourage you to reflect, while in others, I leave you to think for yourself. Note that some quotes will be repeated and that not all of the explanations are based off of the philosophical view of Socrates himself but are from the perspective of a colleague or friend. In other cases, I will provide a terse explanation for you to reflect upon as how a philosopher would. The point of this is to experience the quotes from all angles and perspectives because, from my personal experience, being playful and open about how one receives the knowledge is what makes philosophy more digestible than being cut and dry about it. Journaling is highly recommended, but it is up to you to see how useful this book can be. Enjoy as a self-study or a quick read as you travel or find yourself in the bathroom. Citations to philosophical texts will be placed next to each quote, but notice that in many cases, a quote can be a general theme of one or many of Plato's dialogues. Please note that the citations are primarily from Plato's dialogues, as much of what we know about Socrates comes from his student Plato. Some of the quotes attributed to Socrates may be paraphrases, as exact wording can vary based on translations. Cheers to your development of thought! May you enjoy these quotes and self-reflections. Εβίβα!

Introduction

Socrates, a classical Greek philosopher, remains one of the most influential figures in Western philosophy. His ideas and methods laid the groundwork for much of Western thought. His teachings and reflections have left an indelible mark on philosophy, encouraging individuals to think critically about life, ethics, and knowledge. Known for his unique approach to teaching and his unyielding quest for truth, Socrates never wrote his ideas down. Instead, his thoughts and philosophies were captured by his students, most notably Plato. This small book aims to present over 50 of the most impactful quotes accompanied by brief explanations and facts about Socrates.

Chapter 1: On Knowledge and Ignorance

Know thyself. -Plato, *First Alcibiades*

This is an admonishment for self-awareness. Socrates suggests that there is a fundamental importance in understanding one's own nature and mind. To self-examine our thoughts, words, and actions in order to find meaning in our lives, encouraging us to think for ourselves and question whether or not we live with virtue and integrity. By getting to know ourselves, we get to know each other and gain deeper knowledge of our current reality and the truth behind it all. *Gnōthi Seauton*!

I shall never fear or avoid things of which I do not know, whether they may not be good rather than things that I know to be bad. - Plato, *Apology,* 29b-30b

Socrates advocates for not fearing the unknown on the basis that it might be good rather than being fearful of things simply because they are unfamiliar. He suggests that one should be more cautious about things confirmed to be bad rather than avoid or fear things simply out of ignorance or lack of understanding. One should have courage in the face of the unknown and a grounded approach to discerning the good by actively seeking knowledge rather than living under the shadow of unfounded fears. Unlike assuming the worst about the unknown, Socrates promotes inquiry and intellectual discussion as a means to understand what one does not yet know. Question some of your fears and ask yourself if those fears stem from ignorance or a lack of understanding. Are you living under the shadow of these unfounded fears?

People demand freedom of speech to make up for the freedom of thought which they avoid. -Søren Kierkegaard, *Either/Or*, Part I, p. 19

This quote, wonderfully expressed by Søren Kierkegaard, reflects the irony of how we demand one thing only to ignore the importance of another. Though not a straight quote from Socrates himself, this quote stems from Socratic thinking. It is pointing to the ignorance of the individual who is quick to judge and not observe, quick to desire and not appreciate what they already have, and quick to speak and not think about what is said. This explanation in itself is quite an example of this irony.

Strong minds discuss ideas, average minds discuss events, weak minds discuss people. -Plato, *Phaedo & Republic*

Socrates emphasizes the intellectual hierarchy with a preference for discussing philosophical ideas over mere gossip or events, encouraging one to reflect on the nature of their intellectual engagement and conversations. Here, intellectual discourse and critical thinking is implicitly valued over more superficial or shallow types of discussions. In consideration of your inner dialogue with yourself, what kind of conversations do you find yourself in? Do you think about past conversations with people, past experiences, and wanting to change them, or do you contemplate the lessons that stemmed from those past engagements and integrate them into your being? Note that this integration is what will guide you towards true knowledge of yourself and the world around you.

Death may be the greatest of all human blessings. -Plato, *Apology*, 40c-41c

Socrates' exploration of death is rooted in his broader philosophical practice of questioning and seeking knowledge. He argues that fearing death is irrational because it assumes knowledge of what death entails, which no one truly possesses. Socrates proposes that death may be a blessing for two reasons: On one hand, it could be akin to a deep, uninterrupted sleep without dreams, which would be restful. Alternatively, it could be a transition to another place where he could continue his philosophical inquiries in the company of great minds. His claim challenges the common fear of death by suggesting our dread is based on ignorance. Since death is unknown to the living, it may very well be beneficial rather than harmful.

I know that I am intelligent because I know that I know nothing. -Plato, *Apology*, 21d

There is a certain humbleness we aim to achieve when being a vessel for true knowledge. Notice how Socrates' definition of intelligence always goes back to the acknowledgment that he truly knows nothing. It is like a mantra he repeats to his subconscious until it gets engraved so deeply into his personality that it leads him to become recognized as a philosopher. His sense of wonder and curiosity only deepens the more he is willing to admit to the possibility that he knows nothing. Anyone can admit that they do not know everything, but not everyone can admit that they do not know, especially when placed in a situation in which they are the so-called expert on the topic. Even when we think we know everything about something we've done for years, whatever that may be for you, someone else can have a different perspective or technique. Can you humble yourself enough to admit that you do not know when push comes to shove? If so, learn from it. Catch yourself in those moments and see how to use them to humble yourself into true knowledge.

To find yourself, think for yourself. -Plato, *Crito & Phaedo*

This quote remains highly relevant in the contexts of modern education, personal development, and philosophy. It is a call to action against intellectual complacency that encourages ongoing self-reflection and independent inquiry. It underscores the importance of individual thinking as a path to self-discovery. Socrates believes that true knowledge comes from within and must be reached through personal reflection and reasoned dialogue. This notion promotes the idea that one cannot truly understand themselves if their thoughts are solely influenced by external forces.

Independent thinking leads to authenticity and self-awareness. Thus, by advocating for independent thinking, Socrates encourages people to examine their lives and beliefs critically in order to find themselves.

The only true wisdom is in knowing you know nothing. -Plato, *Apology*, 21d

In times of distress, I've found myself overthinking to the point of a headache, trying to figure out things that were out of my control. It is right at that moment that I cannot handle the stress any longer that I finally scream, "I do not know!" and suddenly, my thoughts stand still. This quote highlights Socrates' belief in the importance of recognizing one's own ignorance as the first step toward acquiring true knowledge. In my case, it was also the first step in acquiring peace of mind in a stressful situation. This humility within me to recognize my own ignorance in the situation and let go of the control to try and fix it allowed for the gates of knowledge to open for me to resolve the issue. Instead of obsessing and stressing about the solution, I allowed the solution to come to me. Reflect on a moment when you thought you knew the answer to something, only to jump the gun and bite the bullet too soon, trying to fix it. What can you learn from that moment?

I know you won't believe me, but the highest form of Human Excellence is to question oneself and others. -Plato, *Apology*, 38a

To question everything in our reality is the baseline mindset of a philosopher. Only through questioning everything can we go forth towards true wisdom. This means full acceptance of our ignorance, making the act of questioning ourselves and others the pinnacle of human thought and moral excellence. As we question our ignorance, we move towards expanding our understanding and humbling ourselves towards true knowledge. Then, and only then, the highest potential we can reach becomes a visible point of focus.

There is only one good, knowledge, and one evil, ignorance. - Plato, *Protagoras*

Many can understand that ignorance is bliss until it becomes misery. Socrates speaks to those living in misery due to their ignorance, pushing them to seek knowledge and understanding of their reality. Only through self-reflection and introspection can we be able to break out of fantasy and see the truth. The first step will always be to admit that we simply do not know anything. Knowledge will never come to us if we do not humble ourselves to our own ignorance. To do good, in this case, means to acknowledge this one truth daily. To do bad and fall to the hands of evil means to think we know what we do not know or assume we know everything. It is even worse if we are aware that we do not know, and we still continue to preach as if we do know.

To know is to know that you know nothing. That is the meaning of true knowledge. -Plato, *Apology & Phaedrus*

When we acknowledge our lack of knowledge, it places us at a greater understanding than those who falsely believe they know everything. This quote goes forth to underscore Socrates' conviction that acknowledging one's ignorance is the beginning of wisdom. Look back on a time when admitting you didn't know the answer led to a discovery of true wisdom within the situation. It is always in the moment we least expect to be wrong when we run into a wall and have to reevaluate ourselves.

An unexamined life is not worth living. -Plato, *Apology*, 38a

Socrates believes that self-reflection and examination of one's life and actions are essential for a meaningful existence, an existence where ignorance of oneself doesn't detriment the outcome of one's actions, where acknowledging and humbling oneself to one's ignorance is the result of recognizing the truth of one's existence. This is the kind of truth that can only be experienced once humbled and can never be explained once acknowledged. Once this is known, it can never be unknown, yet after knowing, it can only be experienced in parts, never as a whole, until the day we die.

Wisdom begins in wonder. -Plato, *Theaetetus*, 155d

Wonder is the emotional state triggered by encountering something new, mysterious, or awe-inspiring. It's a driving force for seeking knowledge and understanding by prompting questions about the nature and workings of things. Socrates holds that a sense of wonder and the recognition of one's own ignorance form the foundation of a philosophical mindset. This inquisitiveness leads to questioning and deeper exploration, ultimately contributing to wisdom. Wisdom is more than just accumulated knowledge; it involves a deeper understanding and the ability to apply knowledge judiciously. The sense of wonder initiates the process that develops into wisdom through continuous questioning and learning.

Chapter 2: On Life and Self-Improvement

There is no greater evil one can suffer than to hate reasonable discourse. -Plato, *Phaedo*, 89c-d, *Gorgias*, 482b-486d

Socrates argues that despising or avoiding rational discussion and open debate is a grave moral and intellectual failing. This leads to misunderstandings and conflict when one is unable to express oneself clearly about their thoughts and intentions. To be able to converse without objectifying the other and maintain focus on the issue at hand is what makes for sound thought to unravel without fallacies. To be unable to discuss such things and utilize anger, sadness, or happiness as a means to dance around and avoid the issue tends to be what leads to confusion and misunderstandings. Before expressing any opinion, one must question oneself to ask if the opinion going to be expressed is one that some thought has been placed upon. Thus, the improvement of society first starts with the improvement of oneself to be able to communicate coherently what it is one strives to communicate. How others may react has no meaning to oneself. How one reacts to others holds meaning to grow and develop from for oneself. As long as you are aware of the quality of your communication, how others react shouldn't hold any bearing on your emotional or mental well-being.

Education is the kindling of a flame, not the filling of a vessel. -Plato, *Meno*

It implies that education should awaken and develop an individual's innate potential and passion for learning. The "flame" symbolizes enlightenment, intellectual growth, and the self-perpetuating nature of inquisitiveness, encouraging a passion and eagerness for learning. The metaphor of a "vessel" suggests that the student's role is merely to receive and contain knowledge, much like a vessel filled with water. This approach can be seen as limiting and non-interactive, stressing rote learning over the development of understanding and critical thinking. Socrates believes that knowledge is latent within the student and that it can be brought to light through proper questioning and dialogue. This is a process of stimulating students' minds, encouraging curiosity, critical thought, and the desire for truth and knowledge. It emphasizes that true education is about self-discovery and developing the student's ability to learn and think independently, as a flame that is kindled will then seek out more fuel and continue to burn, representing the ongoing pursuit of knowledge.

No man is capable of causing great harm to another in wide humanity, yet can only cause this to himself. -Plato, *Apology* & *Gorgias*

This is a philosophical stance that each person's ultimate virtue and vice are internally originated. The choices made, whether of virtue or vice, will cause more of an impact on the individual making those choices than on humanity as a whole. This means that the soul of oneself is more profoundly impacted by one's own choices than by any possible impact on the external. Taking accountability for our choices will, in turn, allow us to make more virtuous choices.

Ignoring self-examination and taking no responsibility for oneself will, in turn, make one choose ignorance. In taking a stance towards your own self-improvement, can you reflect on a time you took accountability for your mistake, only to make the same mistake down the line again?

I cannot teach anybody anything. I can only make them think. - Plato, *Theaetetus*

True teaching, according to Socrates, involves fostering critical thinking, not just imparting knowledge. Many wish to speak about what they know, what they have learned, and how someone else can go forth to do the same. This is a form of poison for the one that continues to impart knowledge unconsciously. They are a poison to themselves and a poison to those around them because this is the type of person who pretends to have a conversation with another, only to hijack the conversation, trying to teach and never allowing the other to have a chance to speak.

In a different scenario, consider an individual teaching who does allow the other to speak; they still aim to control how the other learns and thinks about the subject. Manipulation of thought isn't any better than the hijacking of a conversation. Finally, what we aim to do is have a conversation where ideas are questioned and discussed without forcing opinions down someone's throat. We don't aim to teach nor form someone's thoughts for them. To think critically, we aim to help others think for themselves because by doing so, we ourselves improve our own thinking.

The hottest love has the coldest end. -Plato, *Symposium*

The quote reflects on the nature of passionate love, suggesting that relationships that start with intense emotions often face harsh and disappointing conclusions. Highly intense and passionate feelings can be unstable and may eventually lead to burnout, where the initial fervor disappears and disillusionment sets in. It can be seen as a cautionary observation about the balance of emotions in relationships. Socrates, known for his dialectic method and emphasis on moderation, warns against extremes of any kind, including extreme emotions. This thought encourages individuals to reflect on their relationships and to strive for balance, avoiding the extremes that can lead to relational burnout.

"One who is injured ought not to return the injury."

Our moral integrity is in question here. Is it okay to harm another because they have harmed us? Many would jump to agree on an eye for an eye and a tooth for a tooth. An injustice has been committed, so it's only fair that compensation is given to the victim. The moral issue here then rests on reflecting upon the difference between receiving compensation or getting revenge. Socrates emphasizes the importance of moral integrity, suggesting that retaliation or seeking revenge perpetuates a cycle of harm. Fighting fire with fire will only go on to create a bigger fire, a bigger cycle of harm. Many can give an external appearance of not wanting to seek revenge. One can even go forth to proclaim they don't think of wanting revenge, but this is when self-examination truly begins. Is what you say and do in alignment with your thoughts, or do you assume that you don't have to think because there's nothing to reflect upon? There will always be signs and triggers within our body that will never lie to us, but our mind can easily go forth to assume that there is nothing there and ignore those signs and triggers. How aware are you of these signs and triggers? What is it that you say or do that doesn't align with your thoughts that provoke these triggers?

The way to gain a good reputation is to endeavor to be what you desire to appear. -Plato, *Republic*, Book IV

To walk your talk is the simplest way to describe this quote. Is what you say aligned with what you do, bearing the responsibility for your actions and words and how they appear to the external world? Anyone can pretend to be what they appear to be and say to be, but their actions will always contradict their words and appearance. Their thoughts will always manifest their true interests, and their motives will appear to light, no matter whether they are humble or malicious. Thus, Socrates connects genuine action with reputation. Suggesting that true character builds reputation, not mere appearance or pretense. What reputation do you build by how you appear to the world? Is what you say aligned with what you do? Is what you do reflective of how you want to be perceived?

Strong minds discuss ideas, average minds discuss events, weak minds discuss people. -Plato, *Phaedo & Republic*

The quality of thought within our conversations is in question here. When in conversation with others, are our thoughts towards finding a solution or towards ranting about the problem? If you find yourself ranting, please note that this isn't a bad thing. Sometimes, we need to vent and rant away in order to get our thoughts in order because we are emotionally unstable. To ensure the quality of our thoughts, we must ensure the stability of our emotions. Once we find ourselves somewhat stable emotionally, critical thinking can now begin. We must ask questions and add perspectives, even if irrelevant, that help us grasp the whole of the situation. Like a philosophical detective we remain impartial and follow the clues of ignorance towards knowledge.

Let him that would move the world first move himself. -Plato, *Alcibiades*

The quote implies that hypocrisy is the biggest source of ignorance that can exist. To make an impact on this world, one must first make an impact on oneself. The change we wish to see on this planet must first happen within us. We all know of those sayings that have been heard time and time again with different words from different people throughout the ages. In Socrates' case, he aims to convey that self-improvement and personal accountability are prerequisites for bringing about larger change in the world. Only by leading through example can we truly make a difference. Anything less is a hypocrisy.

The soul is purified from delusions by the process of self-examination. -Plato, *Apology,* 38a & *Phaedrus,* 67d-84b

Self-improvement is implied through the process of self-examination. By stripping away false beliefs, we purify our perspective on the belief itself and expand on its truth. We become clear on its purpose and recognize ourselves differently from how we previously saw ourselves. We then refuse to be manipulated into being something we are not because we understand that our development is everchanging. We are never just one belief but an accumulation of beliefs that make up the entirety of who we are. As we continue to self-examine our thoughts, words, and actions, the delusions of the world will no longer have a grasp on us since we're stripping away the false beliefs the world has taught us. We are clear on who we are as individuals and refuse to be manipulated into being something we are not. It is only by knowing who we are to ourselves that we discover who we can become to the world. Only then will true knowledge be all that remains and be all that we are.

Beware the barrenness of a busy life. -Plato, *Apology*

To live a life so unaware of oneself would be Socrates' greatest nightmare in a society. To be in a hurry and never take the time to witness the present moment is no different than a disease. A busy life leads to a life without purpose, like a plant without fruit. A life without purpose would mean a life that was never lived. Reflect on your life and how your actions have brought you to your current moment in time. Can you perceive the fruit of your labor or even the lack of fruit?

It is not living that matters but living rightly. -Plato, *Crito*

Socrates places a high value on living a virtuous and just life over merely seeking to prolong one's existence. He would rather stare death right in the face than humble himself to admit to unjust persecution. Circumstances should never cause our integrity to falter, even when others deem our beliefs incorrect. Headstrong, we should be to face our fate, never backing down from what we believe to be true. Please note that one can only reach this level of integrity after questioning one's own beliefs so profusely that one's thoughts, words, and actions all act in accordance with one's belief of what is right and what is wrong. Having no fear of the consequences of having that belief is a telltale sign of the integrity of our character and the deeper truth that belief holds within us.

Only the extremely ignorant or the extremely intelligent can resist change. -Plato, *Apology, Crito,* & *Republic*

The quote posits that there are two groups of people who resist change: The extremely ignorant and the extremely intelligent. Those who are rigid in their ways due to a lack of knowledge and awareness resist change because they cannot comprehend or envision the benefits of change. Those who profoundly understand the nature of change and see long-term stability as more beneficial or anticipate and adapt their ideas before the masses have little need for further changes. The quote embodies the idea that knowledge on either extreme can influence one's approach to change differently. Change can be a reflection of acknowledging wisdom or an act of ignorance if not well understood. This can also relate to behaviors in contemporary society, where flexibility and adaptability are traits driven by prudent understanding or sheer obliviousness, while resistance can be either calculated or naive.

Be as you wish to seem. -Plato, *Republic & Phaedrus*

This suggests that people should strive to embody the qualities and virtues they wish others to perceive in them rather than merely putting on a facade. It advocates for real virtues over appearances, and it calls upon individuals to genuinely possess the traits they wish to be recognized for. This ensures that one's outward image is a true reflection of their inner self. This aligns with the philosophical concept of integrity; being true to one's principles and consistent in action and character. Integrity implies that there is no disconnect between how one appears and who they truly are. This idea then inherently encourages personal growth and self-improvement. It suggests that individuals should work towards eliminating the disparity between who they are and who they aspire to be.

Remember what is unbecoming to do is also unbecoming to speak of. -Plato, Charmides

To do harm is considered inappropriate. To speak of such things is no different. To sexually harass a woman in plain day is no different than to sexualize her in words in the dead of night. Words and thoughts tend not to be judged as critically as actions. This is a grave misconception, for our thoughts will become our words, and our words will become our actions. Just because you don't do something that's considered inappropriate doesn't make speaking or thinking about it any better.

He is richest who is content with the least, for content is the wealth of nature. -Xenophon, *Memorabilia,* I.6.10 & Plato, *Apology,* 29d-30b

    To have desire reflects a subconscious belief that we lack that which we desire. In a modern world where material wealth is seen as something to desire, it turns out to be that which we desire insinuates the belief of that which we think we lack. So, no matter what you believe of how much you have, it will never be enough because you think you don't have enough. This leads to a dissatisfying, paradoxical life full of lack. Socrates challenges us to acknowledge that those who are rich in spirit are richer than those who are rich in material wealth. To be content with one's own life is more satisfying than the continuous desire to seek something outside of oneself.

He who is unable to live in society, or does not need to because he is sufficient for himself, must either be a beast or a god. -Aristotle, *Politics,* Book I, 1253a

    Socrates highlights the inherent social nature of humans and the need for community and interdependence. This quote, often interpreted from Aristotle's works on polity and ethics, derives from Socratic ideas of community from Plato's dialogues. It begs the question: Is human innate nature of community or of solitude? What are your thoughts? What has been your experience?

If a man is proud of his wealth, he should not be praised until it is known how he employs it. -Plato, *Apology,* 30b & *Republic*, Book I, 331a-d

Material wealth can come and go without care of how it is used. That is very common nowadays without question, but is the use of that wealth one of virtue? The use of wealth, in this case, is in question, whether it is used to help society rise or drown it into oblivion. If you were to gain a large sum of money all of a sudden, it goes without saying that the first things you would get would be to your benefit and those of your family or friends. The idea of using your wealth to help society wouldn't be a thought unless prior contemplations have been established. In what ways can you help society? It doesn't have to be with money. That example was used so you can recognize your ignorance on the subject. Look at Socrates, for example; not all wealth is material. His wealth was the thoughts he left behind and the legacy that still lives on.

An unexamined life is not worth living. -Plato, *Apology,* 38a

Everything that has ever happened in our lives gave a lesson to learn or a wound to remember. Examining these experiences makes us wiser for the day that a similar experience arises in our present reality. Reflect on the lessons or wounds of your life and how they have guided you to improve or make a necessary change. You can also reflect on the wounds of your life and see the greater lessons waiting to be discovered.

Education is the kindling of a flame, not the filling of a vessel. -
Plato, *Meno*

From birth, we are taught how to be, and if we are otherwise, are judged brutely for it. Socrates wants us to understand that education shouldn't be dogmatic ideas passed down and taught to us by those around us, but instead, it is an inner fire of wonder that guides us to find virtue and truth about what is in front of us. On the other hand, Socrates believes education should ignite a passion for inquiry and understanding rather than just the accumulation of facts. Can you question what you believe as facts and embark on a journey that contradicts those beliefs? Some of those beliefs can be facts you've accumulated yet never questioned. Either one of three things will happen: Your belief will become strong, for you realize that the contradiction was weak; your belief will change because the contradiction was strong; or your belief will expand because both your belief and the contradiction were weak by themselves, yet both held a truth towards true wisdom, which by putting them together, you expanded your perspective.

People demand freedom of speech to make up for the freedom of thought which they avoid. -Søren Kierkegaard, *Either/Or*, Part I, p. 19

No explanation, only a contemplative question with a suggestive example. Can you simply reflect on someone who speaks without thinking and talks so much that they sound like a broken record repeating the same old story? Do you do this? Just note that we see this with older individuals who never questioned their beliefs, ideas, or methods of living and go forth stubbornly to enact the same routine, life habits, and behaviors without thinking. It's like living life on autopilot. This first starts in youth and carries over the older we get.

As to marriage or celibacy, let a man take which course he will, he will be sure to repent. -Plato, *Republic*

The quote reflects Socratic irony, suggesting the inevitability of dissatisfaction regardless of personal choices. No matter what it is one chooses to do, the end result will reflect whether one regrets what one did or not. The irony behind this is that either choice can lead to dissatisfying regret. This is why Socrates nudges us towards philosophical contemplation of our life's decisions. Are the choices we make formed from fallible thinking or reasonable thinking? Are we being lazy to think our choices through, or are we in a rush to make a choice? Either case could very well lead to fallible thinking. Take some time to reflect on your life choices and consider whether they have been done out of laziness or out of a hurry.

He who is not contented with what he has, would not be contented with what he would like to have. -Plato, *Gorgias & Phaedo*

This quote speaks to the importance of contentment and the dangers of constant desire for more. It also implies a lack of gratitude for those who are not content with what they have. Reflect on your desires and note which of them keep you from being content with what you have. Is it material desire? A car, a house, a job, money? Is it emotional desire? A spouse, children of your own, or even grandchildren? What desires cause you to have a lack of gratitude for the life you have? If you don't know where to start, start by practicing gratitude for what you do have. The roof over your head. Legs that help you get out of bed and walk. Clean food and water. Accepting your current reality and holding gratitude for it is the first step towards contentment.

Beware the barrenness of a busy life. -Plato, *Apology*

Constant busyness can hinder personal growth and meaningful engagement with life. Socrates advises individuals to seek a balance between action and reflection, suggesting that meaningful activities grounded in purpose are more fulfilling than mere busyness. It emphasizes the value of taking time for self-reflection versus constantly being occupied with tasks that may not contribute to one's overall well-being or spiritual growth. The quote suggests that deeper fulfillment comes not from doing more but from being more thoughtful in our engagements and priorities. In the contemporary context, the quote can serve as a reminder in a world often obsessed with productivity and multitasking. It warns against losing oneself in a hectic schedule without focusing on what truly matters, such as relationships, personal development, and self-awareness.

Chapter 3: On Ethics and Virtue

Virtue does not come from wealth, but wealth, and every other good thing which men have comes from virtue. -Plato, *Republic*, Book I

Socrates places virtue as the foundation of all good things. He suggests that moral excellence is a prerequisite for a meaningful life, implying that those who act out of desire for material gain will never feel satisfaction for anything they accomplish. The origin of where our motivations derive from will define the value of virtue they hold. If our motives are to gain wealth by harming another, the value of virtue in our motives is none. If our motives are to gain wealth by helping another, then the value of virtue in our motives can be considered. What that value is to be will depend on the integrity of our motives, for even when we want to help, not all who help have integrity in what they do. Even when intentions are good, not all good intentions bear wholesome results.

It is not living that matters but living rightly. -Plato, *Crito*

Socrates' philosophy emphasizes the importance of living a life of virtue and moral integrity. True fulfillment and meaning come not from sheer existence but from living in accordance with ethical principles. To Socrates, the soul's well-being is paramount. Ethical misconduct harms the soul, so it is better to suffer injustice than to commit it. For him, the state of the soul was more crucial than avoiding death or discomfort. Socrates upholds the notion of social contracts and duty towards the state, believing that disobedience to the law, even if the law is unjust, would undermine the very fabric of society and his own moral justification. This quote underscores an important aspect of Socratic moral philosophy, where the processes and choices in life reflect an individual's commitment to virtue. Actions defined by integrity contribute to a 'rightly' lived life.

Justice means minding your own business and not meddling with other men's concerns. -Plato, *Republic*, Book IV

Knowing when to involve oneself and when not to involve oneself in other's affairs can make the difference between virtue and vice. To stay out of something that doesn't concern us is fair, but to some individuals, justice means to get involved in something they have nothing to do with. In this quote, Socrates speaks about justice as understanding one's role and responsibilities without unjust interference. Many arguments can be made on "what-if," this, "what-if," that, but these are "what-if" presumptions. The main point is that a bigger injustice can be made just as easily when getting involved than not getting involved.

From the deepest desires often come the deadliest hate. -Plato, *Gorgias*

To desire something and then not get it, only to throw a fit and hold a grudge, is the basis for fallible thinking and the development of ignorance. Hatred towards someone isn't a baseline emotion to experience. It is an accumulation of emotions that have undergone years of oppression and have remained unexpressed. Years of experiencing the same situation, the same abuse, over and over with different people making the same choice, accumulate that emotion. The accumulation of these emotions will intensify the emotion and, thus, generate profound animosity if not understood or managed correctly. Take a look at how you manage your emotions. Your moral integrity will depend on how well you know yourself and how well you understand the imbalance of your emotions.

I cannot teach anybody anything. I can only make them think. - Plato, *Theaetetus*

Socrates emphasizes the importance of self-discovery and critical thinking over rote learning. He understands that true knowledge comes to those who humble themselves to the process of learning. This quote implies that the virtue of humility can only increase in those who find the ignorance of their thoughts, discovering that thoughts that made sense in the past were simply steppingstones to a truer thought towards true wisdom. In turn, this will make our words and actions that of the purest truth since our thoughts are the first manifestations of what we say and do. Harnessing the virtue of humility within our process of learning then becomes the first step to admitting to our ignorance and stepping towards true knowledge.

There is no greater evil one can suffer than to hate reasonable discourse. -Plato, *Phaedo,* 89c-d, *Gorgias,* 482b-486d

The Socratic principle that rational discourse is essential remains highly relevant. In contemporary times, the importance of civil debate and reasoned argument in public discourse is essential for addressing complex societal issues and fostering understanding among diverse viewpoints. Rejecting reasonable discourse implies a refusal to engage in self-reflection and moral examination. For Socrates, such a stance leads to ignorance and moral stagnation, which he considered profoundly detrimental. To hate or shun reasonable discourse means to reject an essential tool for growth and self-examination. This, according to Socratic philosophy, is a serious flaw. It prevents individuals from questioning their moral beliefs, learning, and ultimately achieving wisdom.

When the debate is over, slander becomes the tool of the loser. - Plato, *Gorgias & Republic*

When one participates in genuine debate, the focus is to seek understanding rather than win an argument. Socrates emphasizes the importance of virtuous behavior. Resorting to slander is seen as indicative of someone who has failed to uphold the principles of reason and virtue. A virtuous individual remains respectful. When one can no longer engage in rational discourse and defend their ideas logically, resorting to slander reveals a defeat. It underscores that the person has no substantive argument left and resorts to attacking character instead. Utilizing slander once a debate has concluded suggests a lapse in moral judgment. Socrates often criticizes rhetoricians who use persuasion without regard for truth or virtue, seeing this as a morally inferior approach to genuine philosophical inquiry.

To know is to know that you know nothing. That is the meaning of true knowledge. -Plato, *Apology* & *Phaedrus*

This is closely tied to Socratic irony and natural humility. Reinforcing the necessity of repeatedly having to humble oneself in recognizing one's own ignorance in order to achieve true wisdom. Humility, in this sense, is the highest of virtues to open the gates of knowledge. To think too highly of oneself will only lead to one's own detriment.

He who is not contented with what he has would not be contented with what he would like to have. -Plato, *Gorgias* & *Phaedo*

Before, I asked you to look at this quote from a self-improvement standpoint. Let's look at it as a virtue for self-examination, shall we? This quote teaches the value of contentment and self-sufficiency. Chasing external desires without inner satisfaction leads to unending dissatisfaction. We can find this in individuals who seek external pleasure to calm their inner imbalances. By inner imbalances, I refer to anxieties, depressions, angers, etc., that cause some kind of urge or kneejerk reaction to crave something external. This can range from over consumption of food, television, medicine, caffeine, alcohol, recreational drugs, or activities like sexual interaction, exercise, and even yoga postures and breathwork. Anything that is done as a means to distract oneself from the inner imbalance is being used as an external pleasure rather than an internal pleasure. Please note that some of the things listed above can be used as an internal pleasure of the soul if and only if it is used without attachment. In other words, it's something that you can go for a day or two without having to worry about or have to STRESS about. For example, those attached to the gym or substance abuse experience stress if they do not get their fix. Some people will argue, "But what if they are a personal trainer or yoga instructor?" In the fitness world, if you are doing any kind of exercise to distract yourself from your problems, you are doing more damage than good. I'm not saying not to do exercise or yoga postures. I'm just saying if there is an attachment that is causing you stress if you don't do it, that's a similar response to someone who feels the need to drink alcohol daily.

Envy is the ulcer of the soul. -Plato, Republic, Book I

Of all the seven deadly sins, envy is the most dangerous of all in consideration of self-preservation. It is the only sin that is willing to demoralize itself consciously in order to hurt another. It's combinations of greed, gluttony, wrath, and pride make it a vicious sin without shame to do what must be done while drowning in its own misery. Socrates would label this misery *ignorance*, for whoever is trapped within the crawls of envy can only go forth to trap others into its own misery, thus its own ignorance.

Be as you wish to seem. -Plato, *Republic & Phaedrus*

Socrates advocates for authenticity and integrity, encouraging individuals to align their actions with their values and principles. How do you wish to be seen by those around you? What values and principles does this version of yourself give to the world? A righteous individual or a corrupt individual? Someone who is respectable or someone who is dishonorable? Good, evil, or ignorant?

If a man is proud of his wealth, he should not be praised until it is known how he employs it. -Plato, *Apology,* 30b & *Republic*, Book I, 331a-d

Wealth should be a means to achieve good and virtuous ends. Socrates believes that true virtue and the worth of a person's character are revealed through their actions and intentions rather than their material possessions or superficial accolades. In this view, external markers of success require scrutiny to determine their true value based on their ethical use. Wealth itself is not inherently praiseworthy; how it is used is what determines its moral value. Employing wealth in a manner that contributes to societal good, justice, and the well-being of others are but a few examples.

He is richest who is content with the least, for content is the wealth of nature. -Xenophon, *Memorabilia,* I.6.10 & Plato, *Apology,* 29d-30b

Socrates taught that a virtuous and contemplative life leads to true happiness and riches. True happiness then stems from inner contentment rather than external wealth, making contentment itself a natural wealth because it does not rely on external circumstances. For Socrates, wisdom and virtue, which he often sees as intertwined, are the highest achievements, far superior to material wealth. The philosophical belief here is that those who are content with little are truly wise because their contentment signifies a deep understanding of what is truly valuable in life. The idea that contentment is an innate wealth of nature reinforces the belief that contentment is an intrinsic state that arises from living a good life. It is not dependent on external factors, which can be volatile and ephemeral. In contemporary society, this insight aligns with modern movements such as minimalism, where simplicity and non-material contentment are highly valued. It also ties into psychological and philosophical discussions about well-being, suggesting that those who manage their desires and find joy in less are often the most content and least stressed. Through this quote, Socrates encourages us to reflect on a life focused on virtue, simplicity, and inner peace as the truest forms of wealth.

He who is unable to live in society or does not need to because he is sufficient for himself must either be a beast or a god. -Aristotle, *Politics*, Book I, 1253a

In this modern day and age, many find themselves wanting to fit in, only to be left disappointed by their community. They attempt to fill a void by pretending to fit in so as to be accepted by others at the cost of never truly accepting themselves. Pretending to fit in will only lead to a lack of integrity in the individual's moral values and authentic nature. External validation then controls the individual's moral value, thereby rejecting their authentic nature, thus rejecting themselves. Community is important, but now, more than ever, the correct community is just as important. A community that we dilute our authentic nature to will only cause us to fall into solitude. To continue in that community then means a continuous delusion of who we are. Can you recall a time you tried to fit in where you didn't belong simply because you did not want to be alone? What did you learn from this?

> *The way to gain a good reputation is to endeavor to be what you desire to appear.* -Plato, *Republic*, Book IV

An underrated virtue in today's society is the act of taking accountability for our actions and words. The words we say and the actions that follow form the character that our reputation is built upon. Who we present ourselves to be to the world is in our complete control. How aware we are of that control can vary, but it depends solely on how genuinely our actions align with our thoughts and the words that follow those thoughts. Mere appearance and words of grace with no actions to back them up are, but mere pretenses to what one's true nature is within. Whether that be with ignorance or without virtue, the question that you must then ask yourself is: What pretenses do I enact to the world?

> *One who is injured ought not to return the injury, for on no account can it be right to do an injustice.* -Plato, *Crito*, 49c-d

Socrates maintains that committing injustice in response to injustice is never right. He argues for an absolute moral principle that one ought not to do wrong, regardless of the wrongs done to them. Socrates is seen as a proponent of moral absolutism, the belief that certain actions are intrinsically right or wrong regardless of context or circumstances. This perspective holds that ethical principles are universally applicable. The principle of not returning injury for injury aligns with later ethical systems, including Christian teachings about turning the other cheek and more contemporary views on nonviolent resistance championed by leaders like Mahatma Gandhi and Martin Luther King Jr. The discussion also brings into focus the critical importance of personal integrity and the idea that one's actions should be guided by ethical considerations, not by expediency or the desire for revenge.

False words are not only evil in themselves, but they infect the soul with evil. -Plato, *Phaedo,* 91a

Socrates cautions against dishonesty, stressing its corrupting influence on integrity. Integrity is the foundation of our virtues and what we base our moral choices on. To lie no matter how big or small, or hide truths regarding the wholeness of a situation leads to a weak foundation of integrity. Moral choices will then depend on what is more convenient at the moment versus what is right and virtuous. This is seen during moments when two vehicles find themselves in a crash, and both individuals claim to be innocent. Though that possibility can exist when one of the individuals is ignorant of their guilt, the majority of the time, one individual knows that they're at fault, but they choose to avoid taking responsibility.

The soul is purified from delusions by the process of self-examination. -Plato, *Apology,* 38a & *Phaedrus,* 67d-84b

For Socrates, the "soul" represents an individual's true essence, which must be purified from ignorance and moral corruption. He believes that without examining one's life and thoughts, individuals remain trapped in false beliefs and unexamined routines. The process of self-examination reveals the biases and misconceptions that cloud moral judgment. This then helps to identify and discard false beliefs, thereby purifying the soul and aligning oneself with truth and virtue. By actively reflecting on one's life, individuals can strive for an ethical existence grounded in truth rather than delusion.

Remember what is unbecoming to do is also unbecoming to speak of. -Plato, Charmides

The quote stresses the importance of integrity and consistency between actions and speech. Socrates frequently emphasizes virtue and ethical behavior. Living a virtuous life involves not only avoiding unethical actions but also abstaining from discussing or endorsing unethical behaviors. What you talk about reflects who you are. Engaging in conversations about things that are unbecoming lowers one's moral standing just as much as actually engaging in such behaviors. It's a reminder to maintain ethical speech to uphold personal and societal moral standards. By advocating for both ethical actions and ethical speech, Socrates is promoting a more virtuous community and encouraging individuals to align their thoughts, words, and deeds with moral principles.

No man is capable of causing great harm to another in wide humanity, yet can only cause this to himself. -Plato, *Apology* & *Gorgias*

This perspective fosters personal resilience by teaching that we are not victims of our circumstances but masters of our internal responses. It empowers individuals to focus on virtue and self-improvement rather than external blame. It places moral responsibility squarely on the individual, suggesting that everyone has the power to maintain their integrity and virtue despite external challenges. Understanding that distress is self-inflicted can help alleviate unnecessary suffering. This insight is particularly relevant in cognitive-behavioral therapies that trace their roots to Stoic principles. If individuals can't be truly harmed by others, it encourages a form of detachment that can change the nature of interpersonal conflicts and lead to more peaceful resolutions.

An unexamined life is not worth living. -Plato, *Apology,* 38a

Before, I described this quote as one of self-improvement, but here, I aim to expand on the perspective of how continuing one's pursuit to improve oneself is a virtue to have. In many quotes, Socrates insists on the importance of self-reflection, believing that examining one's life and actions leads to a more fulfilling and virtuous existence. That's why in examining ourselves, by removing ourselves from the situation, we can help ourselves to see things more objectively. In other words, imagine any situation as if someone else would do what you have done, say what you have said, and think what you have thought. By removing ourselves from the situation, we can examine it more objectively and avoid any of the subjective loopholes we tend to overlook or undermine due to personal interest. If someone else were to do what you have done towards yourself or another, would you still deem it okay? Beware of false sympathy. Since I've asked you to imagine someone else in the situation, it might help to imagine someone you don't like so you don't give them false sympathy or the benefit of the doubt due to you still wanting to justify yourself. This is just something to think about. Having virtue also means acknowledging your own BS and noticing that which you want to deny.

Chapter 4: On Love and Relationships

The hottest love has the coldest end. -Plato, *Symposium*

At first glance, falling in love seems ridiculous to an objective outsider. The experience is quite subjective in nature, and one can't get a taste until engulfed by the experience itself. Socrates makes a point to be wary of that experience and the zeal felt at the start of any new relationship, especially those of romance. The start of a romance is always an exciting occurrence, yet the majority of the time, rational thinking is thrown out the window. This causes one to ignore potential red flags in the relationship, red flags that become more apparent down the line when separation becomes inconvenient due to marriage or children. Before making any choice that has to do with someone entering your life, make sure that you enjoy the beginning stages but don't get lost in any fantasies you craft in your head. You will find more inner peace in seeing who the person is from the get-go than finding out the hard way down the road. Remember that we all show our truest selves at the beginning of a relationship, even if it is sprinkled with a smile and kind words.

From the deepest desires often come the deadliest hate. -Plato, *Gorgias*

Intense passions can generate profound animosity if not understood or managed correctly. In these situations, we must consider our relationship with those around us and how we define and establish those relations. Are we authentically ourselves, or are we pretending to be someone we are not in order to fit in? If we pretend to be something we are not in order to fit in, animosity is guaranteed to be generated over time. If we are authentically ourselves, then only contentment will flourish from those relationships the more they are maintained.

To find yourself, think for yourself. -Plato, *Crito & Phaedo*

Like how many depend on others to love them when they don't want to love themselves, many depend on others to think for them because they don't want to think for themselves. Quite an ironic dilemma when you find yourself in it, but this is both the beginning and end of ignorance for many who suffer throughout their life. Here, Socrates encourages us to take responsibility for our life and hold ourselves accountable for how it develops. By no means does this mean that we shouldn't ask for help or support from others. If you need help, ask for it, but once you have received it, ask yourself if that was the help you needed. By doing so, you find yourself thinking for yourself and accepting what is meant for you, regardless of what others assume to be right for you. You will then find yourself in a state of mind, realizing whether it's your choice to do what you do or not.

Sometimes you put walls up not to keep people out, but to see who cares enough to break them down. -Plato, *Lysis & Symposium*

The quote speaks to the human tendency to create barriers or emotional defenses. These metaphorical walls are put up as self-protection mechanisms due to fear, past hurt, or insecurity. It implies that these barriers serve as tests to identify who values the relationship sufficiently to make the effort needed to overcome them. This then highlights a belief that genuine relationships or friendships require effort and persistence. Those who care enough to persist signify their underlying commitment and sincerity. Thus, Socrates advocates that defenses are not just barriers but measures to test true intentions and alliances.

Be slow to fall into friendship; but when you are in, continue firm and constant. -Plato, *Lysis*

True friendship should be approached with caution and maintained with steadfast loyalty and trust. Socrates, renowned for his methods of self-examination and inquiry, would go forth to ask himself whether or not it is worth it to have someone as a close friend. The same we should do when considering any long-term relationship whether platonic or romantic. This will assure us whether or not it is a relation we wish to have. Ever jumped into a friendship only to find out that the person was only seeking to use you? People will show you at the start of a relationship who they are and what they intend for you. The question is, can you see the truth in front of you, or are you blinded by the fantasy inside of you?

Think not those faithful who praise all thy words and actions; but those who kindly reprove thy faults. -Plato, *Laches,* 187e, *Gorgias,* 458a

This quote expresses a profound belief in the importance of genuine friendship and constructive criticism in personal growth. Socrates distinguishes between superficial flattery and genuine loyalty. He warns that people who incessantly praise every word and action might not have one's best interests at heart. Instead, those who are truly faithful are willing to confront and correct us, even if it might be uncomfortable or difficult. They do so because they care about our well-being and development. In our daily lives, we should value and seek out relationships and environments where honest feedback is encouraged. Embracing such input helps cultivate wisdom, self-awareness, and moral integrity.

Strong minds discuss ideas, average minds discuss events, weak minds discuss people. -Plato, *Phaedo & Republic*

Beware of those you surround yourself with, for their content of thought is what you will fill your mind with. Socrates aims to say that the quality of your thought can only go as far as those you associate with and in the type of discussions you share. Make a list of people that you discuss ideas with, events with, and people with. What is the quality of those relationships in your life? How do they affect you?

Get not your friends by bare compliments but by giving them sensible tokens of your love. -Plato, *Lysis*

Pretty words can be said by anyone. Take this book for example, it is filled by them! Though the words sound nice, are you able to feel the truth and wisdom behind them? The same goes for those who compliment us but leave us feeling drained or icky after encountering them. Socrates would agree that true friendships are built on authentic actions that reflect genuine care, respect, and appreciation rather than hollow compliments or insincere gestures. In those who we seek to have a long-term friendship with, we should consider whether their words are empty or filled. If empty, we will feel drained. If filled, we must then consider the content of the encounter and ask, "Do I feel fulfilled or icky?"

Envy is the ulcer of the soul. -Plato, Republic, Book I

Envy, or in its' immature state, jealousy, is something to be wary of within oneself and those around. Being the most shameless and vicious sin once it has matured, it is a sin that, when worse comes to worst, will do anything in its power to get what it wants. Whether that means harming oneself or harming another, the ignorance of the individual under the delusion of envy can be detrimental all around. Whoever is trapped within the claws of envy can only go forth to harm others due to their own ignorance. Be wary of those who victimize themselves or who are not grateful or content with what they have. Envy tends to be a home for those kinds of people.

False words are not only evil in themselves, but they infect the soul with evil. -Plato, *Phaedo,* 91a

Socrates cautions against dishonesty, stressing its corrupting influence on the liar's and listener's integrity. This can be seen in couples who like to hide truths or tell white lies to each other that later on get discovered. Though it may have been a tiny detail that was purposefully left out or a small lie to avoid conflict at the moment, does not matter. The fact that something was hidden reflects a lack of integrity in one's moral choices. The liar lacks integrity for telling a lie, while the listener lacks it for believing the lie and choosing to stay in the relationship after knowing that they've been lied to in the past. This type of relationship dynamic tends to be a type of cat-and-mouse game, placing both individual's integrity on the line. After a while, the role switches on who chases who, and a different lie is unraveled, causing a toxic cycle to perpetuate back and forth. Can you catch yourself in the moments when you lie, even if it is a white lie? Do you have the moral integrity and humility to take responsibility for the lies you have told?

By all means, marry; if you get a good wife, you'll become happy; if you get a bad one, you'll become a philosopher. -Plato, *Symposium*

Socrates employs humor to underline the unpredictable outcomes of life choices and how challenges foster philosophical reasoning. He depicts the unpredictable nature of marriage, suggesting that any outcome can contribute to personal growth. It implies that difficult experiences, such as those potentially found in a challenging marriage, can promote self-examination and philosophical thinking. Adversities in marriage can then be depicted as catalysts for personal and intellectual growth. Whether one finds happiness or challenge in marriage, both outcomes are presented as opportunities for development. A good marriage brings happiness, while a difficult one encourages philosophical inquiry and wisdom.

Chapter 5: On Courage and Strength

I shall never fear or avoid things of which I do not know, whether they may not be good rather than things that I know to be bad. - Plato, *Apology*, 29b-c

Socrates describes the unknown as something to acknowledge rather than to fear or avoid. Whether we are aware something isn't good or not matters not in any case. To not know something is good doesn't make it bad. To assume that it is bad not knowing if it is good leads to false presumptions. Socrates encourages one to have a curious nature to the unknown instead of a presumptuous one. Whether to fear or avoid something is to fall to ignorance without proof that what we are avoiding or fearing is true. The truth will only be unraveled if we have the courage to stand firm and the curiosity to seek it within every moment that we live.

Wisdom begins in wonder. -Plato, *Theaetetus*, 155d

Many who wander are confused for those who are lost. To be lost means that you don't know where you are going and need help. To wander means you don't know where you are going, but you don't need help to figure it out. As a wanderer, you become familiar with embracing the unknown. This embrace is what allows the unknown to unravel before you. Everything that Socrates has ever thought about came from a space of wonder, a space filled with innocent, unadulterated curiosity for the unknown. By courageously embracing the unknown fully, even when we fear it, true wisdom is the result of that embrace. True knowledge then becomes the unraveling of the unknown.

To find yourself, think for yourself. -Plato, *Crito & Phaedo*

Socrates advocates for independent thinking as a form of strength. Relying on one's reasoning and judgement rather than conforming to societal norms requires courage. This autonomy leads to authentic self-discovery and empowerment, which requires letting go of any dogmatic beliefs and holding firm to the fact that only you can take responsibility for what you think and how you develop.

Not life, but good life, is to be chiefly valued. -Plato, *Crito,* 48b

The quality and morality of one's life are more important than mere existence. Socrates wants us to acknowledge that to have a purposeful life, the quality of how we live matters. Our choices shouldn't depend on external factors or life circumstances. We shouldn't falter to fear or desire. Instead, we should find a solution in which we can live without shame afterwards. For to live without regret and to live with integrity means to stand up even when everyone else chooses to stay down. The fear of being judged by others shouldn't control our integrity. The desire to be accepted by others shouldn't waver our will to live an ethical life. How we spend our days makes a difference in how we feel about our existence. Do you spend your days living in fear? In desire? Or can you stop BS-ing yourself and have the courage to live authentically with integrity?

Bad men live that they may eat and drink, whereas good men eat and drink that they may live. -Plato, *Phaedrus & Republic*

This excerpt differentiates between those who live prudently with purpose and those who live solely for physical pleasures. In recognizing the difference, it is a constant challenge to one's ethical integrity. This challenge serves as a reminder of our values and disciplines. Giving us a point of reference to examine our lives objectively. It also gives us a point of reference to the direction of our purpose. No one truly knows what their purpose entails, but one's actions speak volumes about where their purpose takes them. Having the courage to discern between living with purpose or without grants us a form of strength. A strength that, no matter the circumstance, we choose to live with the values of truth, virtue, and discernment.

True wisdom comes to each of us when we realize how little we understand about life, ourselves, and the world around us. -Plato, *Apology*

Acknowledging one's ignorance requires immense courage. Socrates believes that admitting our limitations is the first step toward gaining true knowledge. This humility and bravery to confront our lack of understanding are the foundations of intellectual strength. Reflect on the last conversation you had and if, within that conversation, you thought you knew something that you actually did not. Whether or not the other individual knew of your ignorance, can you acknowledge that which you did not know? Can you have the continuous courage to acknowledge this every time that it occurs?

Sometimes, you put walls up not to keep people out but to see who cares enough to break them down. -Plato, *Lysis & Symposium*

To anyone who may have been or still is a people pleaser, know that this quote speaks volumes on the importance of setting proper boundaries with the people around you. For example, it is important to be able to say "no" before a time comes when you have an accumulation of oppressed emotions that will explode. Acknowledge that as scary as it may seem, standing firm on saying "no" is an act of love and integrity for yourself and your mental peace, but also towards the individual that you are saying "no" to. To say "yes" when you want to say "no" means that you are lying to that individual. This also implies that you are lying to yourself by not being honest with yourself about how you feel. Be strong enough to be honest with yourself and those around you. Set that boundary because your integrity, your mental state, even your soul is in jeopardy. To your surprise, once that boundary is set, that individual might never bother you again.

False words are not only evil in themselves, but they infect the soul with evil. -Plato, *Phaedo,* 91a

To be truthful with others can feel like the scariest thing to do. Yet to avoid telling the truth or the full truth can have its consequences on our mental well-being. Arrogance and pride might stop many from telling the truth, while in others, it is only the fear of the consequences. Know that telling the truth is a kind of strength and courage many lack. There is integrity in being a light of honesty versus someone who follows the crowd with their lying disharmonies. This will also assure that we live a life without regret because by letting go of the baggage of our dishonesty, we gain liberation from societal disharmonies.

The shortest and surest way to live with honor in the world is to be, in reality, what we would appear to be. -Plato, *Charmides & Apology*

The quote emphasizes the importance of aligning one's inner character with outward appearance. Socrates proposes that true virtue and honor arise not from perceptions or pretenses but from genuinely embodying the qualities we wish others to see in us. Due to social expectations and standards, many are inauthentic about how they wish to be seen by others. To Socrates, it is a virtue to be true to oneself about who they are and how they present themselves to the world. To be courageous enough to follow one's beliefs, even with those who disagree with them, reflects on one's own strength and honor towards their integrity and character. As long as that character is sustained through personal authenticity and authentic goodness, a courageous and virtuous life naturally presents itself. True honor, regardless of whether one is in public or private, is sustained based on one's strength to maintain genuine virtue in who they are.

When the debate is over, slander becomes the tool of the loser. - Plato, *Gorgias* & *Republic*

Acknowledge the fact that a sore loser will always exist, and take it as a lesson of strength and humility. Anger and frustration will be the first emotions most feel when someone starts to throw a fit like a toddler due to being humiliated. Note that this will only bring more humiliation down the line for that individual. Anyone who surrounds them that has a clear sense of the situation will regard their disrespectful behavior as proof of their arrogance. May this acknowledgement give you strength, but be sure not to let it get to your head by assuming you are better than them by being the better person. Allow it to humble you, otherwise you will meet the same fate as them.

The soul is purified from delusions by the process of self-examination. -Plato, *Apology* & *Phaedrus*

Self-examination helps strip away false beliefs, leading to a purer understanding. At times, this can very well be the scariest part of embarking on this journey of self-examination. Do we have the strength and courage to question every belief we hold without giving any of them the benefit of the doubt. Can you recall any beliefs given to you by your parents that led them to say that this is it and that there was nothing else to think about? This tends to be the case when a father wants their child to follow in their footsteps into a career that the father is in, whether it be a doctor, lawyer, police officer, farmer, business CEO, etc. A great example is the original Buddha, whose father wanted him to be a great emperor instead of a great sage. The moral of the story is that the soul will always be surrounded by delusions and expectations from others. Will you have the strength and courage to break out of those delusions and decline those expectations, thus purifying yourself from ignorance and following the truth of your soul? The purest knowledge you can ever retrieve comes from the soul.

Think not those faithful who praise all thy words and actions, but those who kindly reprove thy faults. -Plato, *Laches,* 187e, *Gorgias,* 458a

To our unsatisfying surprise, there will always be those who stand by our side only during the time of our greatest achievements. Once the fame of our achievements is over, suddenly, the attention we once received is gone. The praise that was once given without thought is now denied without a second thought. Our rise now becomes a fall, leaving us no different (or worse at times) than how we started. Though, what remains? The experience of having had experienced what we lived, the lessons that followed those experiences and the people we met, the courage of what it took to rise, and with time, the strength we gained through the experience as it fell down. For what goes up at one point must come down. Majority of the time, who remains won't be those who praised us without thought.

Chapter 6: On Death and the Immortality of the Soul

The end of life is to be like God, and the soul following God will be like Him. -Plato, *Republic & Phaedo*

Socrates views death not as an end but as a potential new beginning, whereby he questions common fears of the afterlife. In this quote, he suggests that as human beings, the ultimate purpose is to emulate the divine nature through virtuous living, making it so that we strive to be the highest of human excellence by assuming the infallible virtue of God. To emulate God on Earth while remaining humble to the fact that it is impossible, we strive to gain the highest of all virtues on Earth to then carry them on to a new beginning the day we die.

To fear death is to think oneself wise when one is not. -Plato, *Apology,* 29a-b

Socrates explains that fearing death presupposes knowledge of the unknown, which is arrogant folly. His perspective on the common fear of death is that it is rooted in a false sense of wisdom. Socrates believes that fearing death implies that one believes they know for certain that death is a bad thing, which is a form of pretending to possess knowledge one does not actually have. Socrates argues that since no one really knows what happens after death, fearing it presumes a negative understanding that cannot be justified by actual knowledge.

The hour of departure has arrived and we go our ways; I to die, and you to live. Which is better? Only God knows. -Plato, *Apology*, 42a

In the dialogue *Apology* by Plato, Socrates finds himself in front of a judge ready to prosecute him with the penalty of death. He was brought to trial on charges of impiety and for corrupting the youth. This corruption involved him teaching the youth to think for themselves and to think critically about what it means to live. In accepting his fate calmly and philosophically, he said the above quote as to describe why he didn't seem to fear death. By doing so, Socrates beautifully describes his belief in the unknown nature of death's potential goodness. He urges us to acknowledge our ignorance of the fact that we don't truly know if death is bad or if death is actually good; we just know that it is inevitable. Why do we fear to live or live in fear because of death? It kind of sounds stupid if you think about it. Why not just love to live or live to love?

Death may be the greatest of all human blessings. -Plato, *Apology*, 40c-41c

Socrates views death not as something to fear but as a natural part of life. By embracing the inevitability of death, individuals can live more fully and fearlessly. This perspective transforms death from a source of dread into a potential blessing, as it liberates the mind from the fear of the unknown. In line with Greek beliefs about the immortality of the soul, Socrates posits that death might not be an end but a transformation. This aligns with his belief in the potential for continued existence and reasoning beyond physical life.

No one knows whether death may not be the greatest of all blessings for a man, yet men fear it as if they knew that it is the greatest of evils. -Plato, *Apology,* 29a

Socrates challenges the common fear of death, suggesting that it is irrational to fear something unknown. He posits that since no one can definitively say what death entails, it might be an extraordinary experience. He proposes that death could be beneficial in ways people do not realize. It might be an end to suffering or a transition to a different state of being, which could be rewarding. This thought encourages a fearless approach to life and a philosophical acceptance of morality, suggesting that how one lives is more important than what supposedly happens after death.

Chapter 7: On God and the Divine Order

Many philosophical discussions led by Socrates involve critical evaluations and reasoned faith in divine order, elucidated broadly in dialogues by Plato such as *Apology*, *Crito*, *Phaedo*, and *Republic*. This allegiance to divine wisdom underscores Socrates' notions of piety, ethics, and existential reflections.

I'm very conscious that I am not wise at all ... but, you see, neither are you. Actually, none of us knows about the gods and their purposes, but all of us pretend that we do. -Plato, *Apology*, 23d

Here, Socrates highlights human limitations in understanding divine matters. He repeatedly acknowledges his own ignorance, a stance that contrasts sharply with the pretenses of those who claim to fully grasp the Divine's will. Socrates' wise ignorance—knowing what he does not know—serves as a critique of both religious dogmatism and human presumption, underscoring a central theme in his philosophy: The unexamined life and the necessity of continuous questioning. This humility before the Divine suggests that true wisdom involves recognizing and respecting the limits of human knowledge in the face of divine mysteries.

I tell you that to let no day pass without talking of the good life and examining both myself and others is really the very best thing a

man can do—and that life without this sort of examination is not worth living. -Plato, *Apology,* 38a

Socrates integrates divine orders with moral and existential examinations of life. He links his philosophy directly to divine duty, emphasizing that his life of questioning, dialogue, and self-examination is guided by a divine mission. He believes that the gods want humans to cultivate their souls through the pursuit of virtue and the good life, asserting that philosophical inquiry is a form of divine service. Socrates considers it his holy mission to challenge and awaken his fellow citizens to greater awareness and moral acumen, thus intertwining human self-improvement with obedience to the Divine's will.

Does not even a doubter believe it is better to obey the gods than to heed men? -Plato, *Crito,* 45c-50a

Socrates advocates for divine law over human law, expressing the inherent superiority and authoritative guidance of Divine Commandments. He argues that moral imperatives delivered through divine channels possess a higher authority than those constructed by humans. The Divine Commandments represent a form of moral truth and justice that transcends human understanding. This conviction leads Socrates to often place himself in opposition to societal norms when they conflict with what he perceives as divinely ordained moral truths.

I am more than convinced that I know nothing but this also, that I know how much I do not know. Therefore, duty is my potion, and to

live, if possible, correctly virtue: To displease God divine justice politics are essentials... -Plato, *Gorgias*

Socrates reiterates his foundational stance on recognizing his ignorance, positioning it as a starting point for his ethical life. He aligns human duties and virtues with divine justice, suggesting that living virtuously is an expression of divine order. By living a life of virtue—one which strives to understand justice, practice it, and fulfill one's responsibilities—humans honor the Divine. This statement reflects Socrates' intricate connection between ethics and divine expectation, intertwining human duty with the Divine's intent.

Before, therefore, we begin any organic discussion, sound, or theme, let us, for good measure, set it as certain: Sacred good derives from the supreme. -Plato, *Phaedrus*, 252b–253c

Socrates insists on framing philosophical discussions within the context of divine belief, asserting that all appreciable moral goods have a sacred origin. The supreme divine entities provide a measure of moral goodness and truth that human endeavors must anchor upon. This insistence on divine foundations suggests Socrates' view that knowledge of ethical truths is also a participation in a higher divine wisdom, underscoring an appeal to a higher, God-given order.

The gods know the just and the unjust, and they are our guides. Let us, therefore, follow them. -Plato, *Gorgias, Republic, Euthyphro,* 9e-15a

This quote underscores Socrates' conviction that the gods possess ultimate knowledge of what is just and unjust. Thus, human beings should adopt the gods as their moral guides, advocating for divine wisdom as a moral compass. According to him, divine intelligence is perfect and omniscient, encompassing the entire moral spectrum. Following the Divine's commands is, therefore, the surest path to justice and the rejection of human fallibility.

We must cultivate the soul and follow the god wherever he leads, allowing ourselves to be absorbed in His divine disclosures. -Plato, *Republic*, Book X

Socrates emphasizes the *imitatio dei* (imitation of the Divine), stating our lives should resemble the pursuit and alignment with godly wisdom and actions. For Socrates, divine guidance provides the pathway to personal and communal improvement. He advocates for soul cultivation, a form of moral development achieved through embracing divine direction. Here, followers internalize divine teachings and let these principles govern their lives, pushing towards moral egalitarianism and spiritual progress, essentially integrating the intellectual quest with spiritual devotions.

The Oracle of Delphi pronounced me the wisest of men, undoubtedly because I am deeply aware that I know nothing. -Plato, *Apology*, 21a

This quote underlies the divine validation of Socrates' outlook on wisdom in recognizing ignorance as a divine favor leading to greater humility and truth pursuit. The Oracle of Delphi, declaring Socrates the wisest due to his awareness of his own ignorance, underscores a divine endorsement of his philosophical method. This seemingly paradoxical wisdom highlights humility as a virtue of the Divine, facilitating recognition of the limitations and complex nature of human understanding of divine wisdom. Socrates interprets this oracle as a mandate to challenge human pretensions of knowledge even further.

No evil can happen to a good man, either in life or after death; he and his will not be neglected by the gods. -Plato, *Apology,* 41d

Socrates expresses his belief in divine providence and protection over righteous individuals. He asserts an inherent cosmic justice guarded by gods who take care of the virtuous both during and afterlife. This divinely assured moral protection implies that the cosmic order, established by the gods, is inherently just. Therefore, physical or temporal suffering are trivial compared to the eternal care and justice provided by divine guardianship.

For I do believe that the gods are concerned with the fate of man and that life and death are noble and ordered well. -Plato, *Phaedo,* 62b-69e

Socrates professes faith in the gods' benevolent guidance over human affairs, including perspectives on birth, life purpose, and mortality. He believes that the gods meticulously oversee human affairs, ensuring that life and death are conducted in an orderly and noble manner. This faith in a divine administration reassures individuals of the inherent dignity in life and beyond. It frames existence within a context of divine order, attributing much of life's unpredictability and complexity to an ultimately benevolent plan of the Divine.

My conviction is that to act justly and to obey the gods is the best way to live. -Plato, *Crito,* 48d

Socrates weds justice to divine obedience. He conveys a unified ethical framework where divine commandments offer the ultimate guide for human behavior. By merging the human duty of justice with strict adherence to divine directives, a life of excellence is achieved. This suggests that true justice aligns with divine decrees, implying that a life led by godly principles is synonymous with just living. This moral guidance provided by divine witness, according to Socrates, is transcendent and remains superior to any human legislation.

Chapter 8: Life and Background

Early Life
Socrates was born around 470/469 BC in Athens, Greece, and died in 399 BC. His father, Sophroniscus, was a stonemason, and his mother, Phaenarete, was a midwife. Unlike many other prominent figures of his time, Socrates did not come from a wealthy family, and he received a basic education in literature, music, and gymnastics, which was typical for Athenian boys of his social class.

Military Service
Socrates served as a hoplite (a heavily armed foot soldier) in the Athenian army. He participated in several significant battles, including the Battle of Potidaea, the Battle of Delium, and the Battle of Amphipolis. His courage and resilience in battle were well-regarded by his contemporaries.

Philosophical Pursuits
Despite his profound influence, Socrates left no writings of his own. Our knowledge of his teachings comes mainly from his students, Plato and Xenophon, and the playwright Aristophanes. He spent much of his life engaging in public debates and discussions in the marketplaces and public spaces of Athens, questioning the moral and philosophical beliefs of his fellow citizens.

Trial and Death

In 399 BCE, Socrates was brought to trial on charges of impiety and corrupting the youth of Athens. He was found guilty and sentenced to death by drinking a cup of poison hemlock. His trial and death are recounted in several works by Plato, most notably in the *Apology*, *Crito*, and *Phaedo*. During his trial, as documented by Plato in *Apology*, Socrates remained steadfast in his beliefs and used the opportunity to teach and challenge the jury's thinking.

Legacy

Socrates' philosophy laid the foundations for ethical deliberations in Western philosophy. His thoughts, theories, and efforts mainly focused on the use of reason towards the service of humanity, questioning human morality, virtue, and what it means to live a good life as a human. He remains a central figure in the study of Western philosophy, and his approaches to ethics, epistemology, and logic continue to be influential.

Philosophical Method

The Socratic Method: Socrates is famous for his dialectical method of teaching. The Socratic Method, also known as *elenchus*, is a form of cooperative argumentative dialogue that Socrates used to stimulate critical thinking and to illuminate ideas. It involves asking and answering questions to stimulate critical thinking and to draw out underlying presumptions. This method remains a fundamental tool in modern education and law.

Connections With Other Philosophers

Socrates was a mentor to many significant philosophers, including Plato, who would later tutor Aristotle. Socrates' dialogues in Plato's works, such as *The Republic* and *Phaedo*, serve as primary sources of his ideas.

Conclusion

The depth and simplicity of Socrates' thoughts and his dedication to relentless questioning have left an indelible mark on philosophy. His teachings encourage us to seek inner contentment, engage in self-reflection, think independently, approach the world with ethical integrity, and acknowledge the natural cycle of life and death. His legacy teaches us to embrace humility, constantly seek knowledge, and live life with integrity and introspection. By internalizing these principles, we can cultivate a stronger and, more courageous, and fulfilling existence.

About the Author

Sebastián was born in Mexico and raised in the United States. Half of the first seven years of his life were spent in silence due to an overgrowth of the frenulum tissue underneath his tongue, restricting his ability to talk. This led him to adapt to a form of wordless communication, causing him to have to think differently than most children his age. Struggling with speech impediments and having to learn English while retaining his Spanish made for the development of an eccentric young man. His interest in philosophy started with his friends in college who, at the time, introduced philosophy to him by engaging in discussions of critical thinking. Though they emulated Plato's Symposium and drank while speaking, it was these moments that left an impression on Sebastián, leading him to consider philosophy as something worth studying. With time, he branched out, learning about the philosophies of different cultures like Hinduism's concept of Yoga, Wicca's concept of witchcraft, and Christianity's concept of the Gospel, only to end up back to where he started with his favorite philosopher. To this day, he acknowledges the fact that after all this time, he may have experienced and learned a lot, but he still finds himself humbled by the words of Socrates, realizing that true knowledge lies beyond the scope of what he knows.

(@shavatian: Instagram & Facebook)

References

Aristotle, Politics, Book 1, section 1253a. (n.d.). Www.perseus.tufts.edu. https://www.perseus.tufts.edu/hopper/text?doc=Perseus%3Atext%3A1999.01.0058%3Abook%3D1%3Asection%3D1253a

Hayward, J., Cardinal, D., & Jones, G. (2007). *The Republic: Plato.* Hodder Murray.

Jones, L., & Gaul, C. C. (1927). *Gems of the world's Best Classics: a collection of complete short stories and essays chosen from the literatures of all periods and countries.* Geographical Pub. Co.

Kierkegaard, S. A. (2021). *Either/Or : Kierkegaard, Søren* (H. V. Hong & E. H. Hong, Eds.). Internet Archive; Princeton, N.J.: Princeton University Press. https://archive.org/details/either-or-part-1-kierkegaards-writings_compress/page/18/mode/2up

Plato, & Bluck, R. S. H. (1955). *Phaedo: The phaedo of Plato translated with introduction, notes, and appendices.* Liberal Arts Press.

Plato, & Denyer, N. (2001). *Plato: Alcibiades.* Cambridge University Press.

Plato, & Fowler, H. N. (1921). *Theaetetus - Sophist.* Harvard University Press; Heinemann.

Plato, & Jowett, B. (2006). *Euthyphro.* Project Gutenberg.

Plato, & Nichols, J. H. (1998). *Gorgias and Phaedrus*. Cornell University Press.

Plato, & Sharon, A. (2015). *Plato's Symposium*. Hackett Publishing Company, Inc.

Plato. (2004). *The Apology*. Nuvision Publications.

Plato. (2005). *Protagoras and Meno*. Penguin Books.

Tuckey, T. G. (1968). *Plato Charmides*. Hakkert.

Xenophon. (2008, August 24). *The Project Gutenberg EBook of The Memorabilia, by Xenophon* (H. G. Dakyns, Ed.). Www.gutenberg.org.
https://www.gutenberg.org/files/1177/1177-h/1177-h.htm

Notes

www.ingramcontent.com/pod-product-compliance
Lightning Source LLC
LaVergne TN
LVHW052048070526
838201LV00086B/5131